Animals Asleep

Sneed B. Collard III

illustrated by

Anik McGrory

Houghton Mifflin Company Boston 2004

To my son, Braden Guy Collard,
my favorite napping buddy
Love, Your Dad

For Glenn, who rocks our baby to sleep
—Anik

Text copyright © 2004 by Sneed B. CollarText copyright © 2004 by Sneed B. Collard III
Illustrations copyright © 2004 by Anik Scannell McGrory

All rights reserved. For information about permission to reproduce
selections from this book, write to Permissions, Houghton Mifflin
Company, 215 Park Avenue South, New York, New York 10003.

www.houghtonmifflinbooks.com

The text of this book is set in 14-point Dante.
The illustrations are watercolor.

Library of Congress Cataloging-in-Publication Data
Collard, Sneed B.
Animals asleep / Sneed B. Collard III ; illustrated by Anik McGrory.
p. cm.
Summary: Provides a look at the many different ways in which animals
sleep, from a snoozing orangutan to a sleeping whale, as well as facts
about each animal pictured.
ISBN 0-618-27697-1 (hardcover)
1. Sleep behavior in animals—Juvenile literature. 2. Animal behavior—
Juvenile literature. [1. Animals—Sleep behavior. 2. Animals—Habits
and behavior.] I. McGrory, Anik, ill. II. Title.
QL755.3.C65 2004   591.56—dc22   2003012413

Printed in Singapore
TWP 10 9 8 7 6 5 4 3 2 1

Most of us need sleep.

Whether it's a snooze...

Orangutans live in the rain forests of Southeast Asia. They are closely related to humans and are earth's largest tree-dwelling animals. An orangutan spends most of its day looking for fruits and other food, but it pauses now and then for a snooze in the trees. Often, before each nap—and before turning in for the night—it weaves a comfortable sleeping nest of branches and leaves.

A nap...

Pandas are some of nature's cutest critters.
They eat bamboo and, like orangutans,
spend much of their lives looking for food.
But they do find time for naps. When they
want to rest, pandas flop down on almost
any soft spot on the ground. Mother pandas
often curl up to nap with their babies.

A doze ...

Snakes spend most of their time resting or sleeping. When a snake isn't looking for a fat mouse to eat or trying to find a mate, it can usually be found coiled up under a log or in another safe place. Snake owners often report that their pets doze off in their laps or inside their shirts. Think about that the next time you reach into someone's pocket!

Or a long winter's dream.

Raccoon dogs live in eastern Asia and Europe. They hunt mainly at night, searching for plants, insects, fish, birds, and other prey to eat. In summer and early fall, they put on as much fat as possible. Then they crawl into caves or dens and sleep until early spring. During this long rest they wake now and then, but they still have plenty of dream time.

Some of us sleep in the day.

Like owls, **tawny frogmouths** hunt at night. They fly slowly or perch in a tree until they see a mouse, frog, or juicy insect. Then they swoop down to seize their meal. During the day, frogmouths sleep on logs and branches. Never seen one? That's not surprising. They live only in Australia, and their gray and brown feathers make them look just like **wood.**

Others, at night.

In a tropical rain forest, sleeping can be hazardous to your health. To make sure a hungry snake doesn't sneak up on it, an **anolis lizard** often sleeps on a leaf at the end of a slender branch. The branch acts like an alarm clock. If a predator accidentally shakes it, the lizard wakes and leaps to safety.

A few sleep whenever we can!

If you have a **cat**, you know what its favorite activity is. Sure, cats eat and play and cuddle and groom, but more than anything else, they sleep. An average cat sleeps about sixteen hours each day. Do you think they're really that tired, or are they just bored?

We can sleep in a bed.

Sea otters make a living by diving for shellfish along the rocky Pacific coast. They rarely come ashore. When it's time to sleep, they just sack out in a nearby kelp bed. Sometimes they'll even wrap themselves in the rubbery, slippery seaweed. The kelp keeps sea otters anchored in place—and helps hide them from sharks swimming below.

A hole.

Woodpeckers often sleep in holes they chip out of diseased or dead trees, called "snags." Many other animals, from wood ducks to bluebirds, take over these nice, roomy apartments. By chipping out sleeping quarters for themselves, woodpeckers provide homes for many other forest species.

Underground.

Tuataras look like lizards, but they belong to their own separate group of reptiles. One hundred million years ago, tuataras lived all over the world. Today they live only in New Zealand. Tuataras sleep underground in burrows dug by petrels and other shorebirds. These slow-moving, gentle reptiles spend much of their lives in these burrows, especially in winter. On warm nights, they come out to mate and hunt for insects and other small, slow-moving prey.

Or, when we need to, up in the air.

Sooty terns usually nest on tropical islands. They spend the rest of the year flying over tropical seas, often hundreds of miles from shore. Without getting wet, the terns pluck fish, squid, and other food from the sea surface. The big question is, where do they sleep? Almost all other birds sleep and rest on land. But bird experts believe that sooty terns sleep or doze in midair as they slowly flap their wings.

Some of us sleep together.

Butterflies often gather together at night to roost. Groups of colorful passion vine butterflies, for instance, spend their nights on rain-forest plants. No one is quite sure why they do this. The butterflies feed on plants that make them taste bad to birds and other predators. By roosting together, they may be creating a big, colorful sign that says, "Don't eat us or you'll be sorry!"

But most sleep all alone.

If you could cross a pig with an elephant, you might end up with an animal that looks like a **tapir**. Tapirs live in the rain forests of Asia and Central and South America and can weigh as much as 640 pounds. Several tapirs may live in the same area, but they tend to be loners. They usually forage for plants, fruits, and seeds by themselves. During the day, they settle down in cool spots on the forest floor to sleep.

We sleep on our backs…

Dogs seem to be able to sleep in almost any position you can think of. They sleep curled up. They sleep on their sides. They even sleep on each other! My favorite is when dogs sleep on their backs with their legs in the air. Do you think this border collie feels silly sleeping this way?

Our stomachs...

Alligators are built like fortresses.
Armored plates and scales cover their
skin and provide good protection
from predators—and other alligators.
Alligators have much more armor
on their backs than on their undersides.
That could explain why you never see
an alligator sleeping belly up.

And sometimes upside down.

Bats are famous for sleeping upside down. In Asia and Australia, huge colonies of beautiful fruit bats called "flying foxes" roost together in coastal forests. The bats are restless sleepers and often seem to wake up and pester their neighbors. At sunset, the bats take off and fill the skies, searching for ripe mangoes, papayas, and other fruits to eat.

Most fish sleep.

You might not think that fish sleep, but most of them do. Brightly-colored **parrotfishes** live on coral reefs. At night, a parrotfish surrounds itself with a mucus "sleeping bag" before bedding down in a hole or crevice. The mucus is released from special pores around the fish's head and slowly surrounds its entire body. Scientists believe that the mucus tastes bad to sharks and other predators, protecting the parrotfish so that it lives to swim another day.

And so do dolphins.

For an air-breathing mammal, sleeping in water could be a problem. Most **whales** and **dolphins** solve this problem by sleeping as they float at the ocean's surface. A bottlenose dolphin, though, can also put half of its brain to sleep at a time. While half of the brain rests, the other half lets the dolphin slowly swim, breathe, and watch over any babies. After a couple of hours, the sleeping half wakes up to let the other half of the dolphin's brain take a snooze.

Do giant clams sleep?
Your guess is as good as mine!

Scientists still don't understand a lot about sleep in **invertebrates**—animals without backbones. Most invertebrates seem to have daily rest periods. A few even release some of the same chemicals into their blood that we do when we're asleep. But is a clam or fly or worm *really* asleep? Scientists will have to do more research to know for sure.

But whenever or wherever or however we do it, most of us need sleep.

Isn't it about time?